Dear little artists,

This coloring book was created especially for you, who love to bring life and color to the world around you. May each page be an exciting adventure, where animals and sports come to life through the colors of your imagination. May each stroke be a moment of joy and learning. May fun and creativity never end!

Dear parents,

With immense gratitude, I dedicate this book to you, who nurture a love for art and movement in your children. Through the simple act of coloring, may they discover a world of possibilities and develop their creativity. Thank you for investing time and love in shaping children who value healthy habits and the beauty of artistic expression. May this book be another tool in your journey of raising happy human beings connected to what truly matters.

With all my respect and admiration,

Marcelo Kobe
Passionate about united families.

This book belongs to:

Name of the artist child!

Parents' names!

TEST COLOR PAGE

Blue

Red

Yellow

Green

Orange

Purple

Brown

Gray

BEAR
JUMPING ROPE

COW
RIDING A ROLLER

HORSE
DRIVING A KART

RHINO
PLAYING HOCKEY

TOUCAN
PRACTICING ARCHERY

CAT
PLAYING BASKETBALL

DOG
PLAYING SOCCER

MONKEY
PLAYING VOLLEYBALL

WHALE
JUMPING WITH PARACHUTE

KOALA
SWIMMING

RABBIT
RUNNING

PIG
PLAYING BASEBALL

PARROT
RIDING A BICYCLE

DUCK
PLAYING BOWLING

BEE
FLYING BY GLIDING WING

ALLIGATOR
SURFING

ELEPHANT
PRACTICING BOXING

HIPPO
SKIING

LION
PRACTICING JUDO

TURTLE
RIDING A SKATEBOARD

WOLF
PLAYING TENNIS

PANDA
WINDSURFING

FROG
TAKING A TRAIL

GIRAFFE
DIVING

ZEBRA
SNOWBOARDING

TIGER
LIFTING WEIGHT

GORILLA
ON KAYAK

DOLPHIN
PLAYING GOLF

PENGUIN
PLAYING AMERICAN FOOTBALL

KANGAROO PLAYING BILLIARDS